10637486

THIS BOOK BELONGS TO

CONTENTS

INTRODUCTION

It is a great privilege to be a son of God! You are important to God, and he wants a special relationship with you. Reading even just a little bit of his Word each day will give you strength and fill you with hope.

Prayers & Promises for Boys is a topically organized collection of God's promises that guide you through lessons of courage, faith, strength, wisdom, honor, and more. Heartfelt prayers and prompting questions give you an opportunity to think more deeply about the promises found in God's Word.

Be encouraged as you sit with God and learn more about the love he has for you!

FRIENDSHIP

A friend loves you all the time,
and a brother helps in time of trouble.

PROVERBS 17:17 NCV

"Greater love has no one than this: to lay down one's
life for one's friends. You are my friends if you do what
I command. I no longer call you servants, because a
servant does not know his master's business. Instead,
I have called you friends, for everything that I learned
from my Father I have made known to you."

JOHN 15:13-15 NIV

There are "friends" who destroy each other,
but a real friend sticks closer than a brother.

PROVERBS 18:24 NLT

"In everything, do to others
what you would want them to do to you."

MATTHEW 7:12 NIRV

Dear God, I love my friends, but I don't know if they know it. It is hard for me to show them how much they are appreciated. I pray that with you as my example, my actions will show my friends that they are a blessing.

What friend can you pray for right now?

HONOR

"My Father will honor the one who serves me."

John 12:26 NIV

Humble yourselves under the mighty power of God,
and at the right time he will lift you up in honor.

1 Peter 5:6 NLT

Anyone who wants to be godly and loving
finds life, success and honor.

Proverbs 21:21 NIRV

Love each other like brothers and sisters. Give each
other more honor than you want for yourselves.

Romans 12:10 NCV

Dear God, you honor me and ask me to honor others. I should put them before myself in honor. Help me to be humble and kind. I want to be more like you every day.

How can you honor someone today?

RESPECT

Show respect for all people: Love the brothers
and sisters of God's family, respect God, honor the king.

1 PETER 2:17 NCV

Trust in your leaders. Put yourselves under their
authority. Do this, because they keep watch over you.
They know they are accountable to God for everything
they do. Do this, so that their work will be a joy. If you
make their work a heavy load, it won't do you any good.

HEBREWS 13:17 NIRV

Don't do anything only to get ahead.
Don't do it because you are proud.
Instead, be humble.
Value others more than yourselves.

PHILIPPIANS 2:3 NIRV

Dear God, sometimes I act rude or disrespectful when I disagree or don't get my way. You say to show respect for all people and to especially respect and obey my leaders, like parents and teachers. Help me to be more respectful to everyone in my life.

How can you show respect today?

WISDOM

Wisdom will come into your mind,
and knowledge will be pleasing to you.
Good sense will protect you;
understanding will guard you
It will keep you from the wicked,
from those whose words are bad.

PROVERBS 2:10-12 NCV

Wisdom and money can get you almost anything,
but only wisdom can save your life.

ECCLESIASTES 7:12 NLT

If any of you needs wisdom, you should ask God for it.
He will give it to you. God gives freely to everyone
and doesn't find fault.

JAMES 1:5 NIRV

Dear God, I hear adults talk about being wise and having wisdom. It's not something I thought I could have. But you say you will give it to me if I ask for it. I want more wisdom so I can live better for you.

How could wisdom help you make better choices?

CARING

Do not be interested only in your own life,
but be interested in the lives of others.

PHILIPPIANS 2:4, NCV

If anyone has material possessions and sees a brother or
sister in need but has no pity on them, how can the love
of God be in that person? Dear children, let us not love
with words or speech but with actions and in truth.

1 JOHN 3:17-18 NIV

"I was hungry. And you gave me something to eat. I was
thirsty. And you gave me something to drink. I was a
stranger. And you invited me in. I needed clothes. And
you gave them to me. I was sick. And you took care of me.
I was in prison. And you came to visit me."

MATTHEW 25:35-36 NIRV

Dear God, I care about my family and my friends.

Help me to be loving and caring like you are,

and not to think only about myself.

How can you care for a friend today?

DILIGENCE

The plans of the diligent lead to profit
as surely as haste leads to poverty.

PROVERBS 21:5 NIV

Work with enthusiasm, as though you were
working for the Lord rather than for people.

EPHESIANS 6:7 NLT

Many good things come from what people say.
And the work of their hands rewards them.

PROVERBS 12:14 NIRV

We must not become tired of doing good.
We will receive our harvest of eternal life
at the right time if we do not give up.

GALATIANS 6:9 NCV

Dear God, chores and homework are not always fun.
You say to work with enthusiasm and to work as if I am
working for you. Help me to be more diligent and to have
a better attitude about working.

What will help you become more enthusiastic about work?

TEMPTATION

The temptations in your life are no different from
what others experience. And God is faithful.
He will not allow the temptation to be more
than you can stand. When you are tempted,
he will show you a way out so that you can endure.

1 Corinthians 10:13 NLT

"Watch and pray so that you will not fall into temptation.
The spirit is willing, but the flesh is weak."

Matthew 26:41 NIV

I have taken your words to heart
so I would not sin against you.

Psalm 119:11 NCV

Dear God, temptations are hard to deal with for everyone, but you say you always give me a way out of the wrong choice. I pray that you help me to do the right thing.

What helps you resist temptation?

STRENGTH

God is our refuge and strength,
an ever-present help in trouble.

PSALM 46:1-3 NIV

The Lord is faithful;
he will strengthen you
and guard you from the evil one.

2 THESSALONIANS 3:3 NIRV

Don't be afraid, for I am with you.
Don't be discouraged, for I am your God.
I will strengthen you and help you.
I will hold you up with my victorious right hand.

ISAIAH 41:10 NLT

Dear God, I feel like I always have to act tough and strong even when I don't feel that way. It is nice to know it's okay to be weak around you because you give me strength. Thank you for keeping me safe.

How does Jesus make you feel stronger?

LEARNING

Those who get wisdom do themselves a favor,
and those who love learning will succeed.

PROVERBS 19:8 NCV

Pay attention to my wisdom;
listen carefully to my wise counsel.
Then you will show discernment,
and your lips will express what you've learned.

PROVERBS 5:1-2 NLT

Hold on to my teaching and don't let it go.
Guard it well, because it is your life.

PROVERBS 4:13 NIRV

Whatever you have learned or received or heard
from me, or seen in me—put it into practice.
And the God of peace will be with you.

PHILIPPIANS 4:9 NIV

Dear God, learning isn't always fun, but I know it is something I need to do. Help me to enjoy the learning that comes from you because it will teach me how you want me to live.

What helps you learn?

HOPE

The LORD is good to those whose hope is in him,
to the one who seeks him.

LAMENTATIONS 3:25 NIV

And hope will never bring us shame. That's because
God's love has poured into our hearts. This happened
through the Holy Spirit, who has been given to us.

ROMANS 5:5 NIRV

The LORD 's delight is in those who fear him,
those who put their hope in his unfailing love.

PSALM 147:11 NLT

Dear God, it's good to have hope in my life. When bad things happen, sometimes I lose hope. Then, I remember you love me and want the best for me. Thank you for that hope.

How does having hope change how you live?

JOY

May the God of hope fill you with all joy and peace as you
trust in him, so that you may overflow with hope by the
power of the Holy Spirit.

ROMANS 15:13 NIV

"Go and enjoy good food and sweet drinks.
Send some to people who have none,
because today is a holy day to the Lord.
Don't be sad, because the joy of the LORD
will make you strong."

NEHEMIAH 8:10 NCV

The LORD is my strength and shield.
I trust him with all my heart.
He helps me, and my heart is filled with joy.
I burst out in songs of thanksgiving.

PSALM 28:7 NLT

Dear God, thank you for joy. Thank you for letting me laugh with my friends and joke with my family. I am happy that I belong to you.

How does God make you joyful?

PATIENCE

Warn those who are lazy.
Encourage those who are timid.
Take tender care of those who are weak.
Be patient with everyone.

1 THESSALONIANS 5:14 NLT

Be like those who through faith and patience
will receive what God has promised.

HEBREWS 6:12 NCV

Be completely humble and gentle;
be patient, bearing with one another in love.

EPHESIANS 4:2 NIV

Anyone who is patient has great understanding.
But anyone who gets angry quickly
shows how foolish they are.

PROVERBS 14:29 NIRV

Dear God, patience is hard to practice, but you value patience over anger. I want to please you and treat others with love. When I feel like getting angry with someone or acting rude, I pray that I will think of you and be patient instead.

What helps you be patient when you get frustrated?

HEALTH

The world and its desires pass away,
but whoever does the will of God lives forever.

1 JOHN 2:17 NIV

Don't be wise in your own eyes.
Have respect for the LORD and avoid evil.
That will bring health to your body.
It will make your bones strong.

PROVERBS 3:7-8 NIRV

I will never forget your commandments,
for by them you give me life.

PSALM 119:93 NLT

A happy heart is like good medicine,
but a broken spirit drains your strength.

PROVERBS 17:22 NCV

Dear God, thank you for the healthy days you have given me. If I keep my heart happy, you say it is good medicine. Help me to keep a happy attitude so I can stay healthy.

How does a happy heart make your body feel?

GUIDANCE

Guide me in your truth and teach me,
for you are God my Savior,
and my hope is in you all day long.

PSALM 25:5 NIV

Wise people can also listen and learn;
even they can find good advice in these words.

PROVERBS 1:5 NCV

We can make our plans,
but the LORD determines our steps.

PROVERBS 16:9 NLT

Those who are led by the Spirit of God
are children of God.

ROMANS 8:14 NIRV

Dear God, I know I need guidance, but sometimes I want to do things my own way. I feel like I don't need help. I shouldn't think like that because you are the best guide, and you teach me how I should live.

How can you let God be your guide today?

GOODNESS

Everything God created is good, and nothing is to be rejected if it is received with thanksgiving.

1 Timothy 4:4 NIV

Taste and see that the Lord is good.
Oh, the joys of those who take refuge in him!

Psalm 34:8 NLT

My brothers and sisters, I am sure that you are full of goodness. I know that you have all the knowledge you need and that you are able to teach each other.

Romans 15:14 NCV

Dear God, it's hard to understand that there is evil in this world when you are so good. I pray that others will see your goodness in me and that I will be a light in the darkness. Thank you for your goodness.

How can you show others God's goodness?

THANKFULNESS

I have not stopped giving thanks for you,
remembering you in my prayers.

EPHESIANS 1:16 NIV

Giving thanks is a sacrifice that truly honors me.
If you keep to my path,
I will reveal to you the salvation of God.

PSALM 50:23 NLT

Rejoice always, pray continually,
give thanks in all circumstances;
for this is God's will for you in Christ Jesus.

1 THESSALONIANS 5:16–18 NIV

Give thanks as you enter the gates of his temple.
Give praise as you enter its courtyards.
Give thanks to him and praise his name.

PSALM 100:4 NIRV

Dear God, you are the reason for everything good in my life. Help me to have a more thankful heart. Thank you for this day, and thank you for my friends and family.

What can you thank God for right now?

RELIABILITY

"All people are like grass. All their glory is like the
flowers in the field. The grass dries up. The flowers fall
to the ground. But the word of the Lord lasts forever."

1 PETER 1:24-25 NIRV

Every good action and every perfect gift is from God.
These good gifts come down from the Creator of the sun,
moon, and stars, who does not change
like their shifting shadows.

JAMES 1:17 NCV

He will give eternal life to those who keep on doing good,
seeking after the glory and honor and immortality that
God offers.

ROMANS 2:7 NLT

Dear God, I know I can rely on you for anything. Nothing else in this world is as dependable as you. You are forever. Help me to get my strength from you every day.

What does it mean for you to be reliable?

EXCELLENCE

Always think about what is true. Think about what is
noble, right and pure. Think about what is lovely and
worthy of respect. If anything is excellent or worthy of
praise, think about those kinds of things.

PHILIPPIANS 4:8 NIRV

Whatever you do, work at it with all your heart,
as working for the Lord.

COLOSSIANS 3:23 NIV

The answer is, if you eat or drink,
or if you do anything,
do it all for the glory of God.

1 CORINTHIANS 10:31 NCV

Dear God, you made me to be excellent and to represent you well. I should be thinking most about things that are good and right. Help me to think and act more like you.

Why do you think excellence is important to God?

BLESSINGS

Surely, LORD, you bless those who do what is right.
Like a shield, your loving care keeps them safe.

PSALM 5:12 NIRV

"But even more blessed are all who hear the word of God
and put it into practice."

LUKE 11:28 NLT

Give praise to the God and Father of our Lord Jesus
Christ. He has blessed us with every spiritual blessing.
Those blessings come from the heavenly world. They
belong to us because we belong to Christ. God chose us to
belong to Christ before the world was created. He chose
us to be holy and without blame in his eyes. He loved us.

EPHESIANS 1:3-4 NIRV

Dear God, you bless those who do the right thing. I want to do the right thing not only for the blessings you give but also just to please you. You chose me to be your son, and I want to do all that I can to live like you.

How has Jesus blessed your life lately?

HUMILITY

"Didn't I make everything by my power? That is how all things were created," announces the LORD. "The people I value are not proud. They are sorry for the wrong things they have done. They have great respect for what I say."

ISAIAH 66:2 NIRV

Humble yourselves before the Lord,
and he will lift you up.

JAMES 4:10 NIV

Pride will ruin people,
but those who are humble will be honored.

PROVERBS 29:23 NCV

The LORD has told you what is good,
and this is what he requires of you:
to do what is right, to love mercy,
and to walk humbly with your God.

MICAH 6:8 NLT

Dear God, I don't want to be prideful, but sometimes I act that way. I want to be kind and humble toward my friends and family. I want them to see you in me. Help me to have more humility.

Can you describe a time when you showed humility instead of pride?

WORRY

Turn your worries over to the LORD.
He will keep you going.
He will never let godly people be shaken.

PSALM 55:22 NIRV

"Who of you by worrying
can add a single hour to your life?"

LUKE 12:25 NIV

Worry weighs a person down;
an encouraging word cheers a person up.

PROVERBS 12:25 NLT

Do not worry about anything, but pray and ask God for
everything you need, always giving thanks. And God's
peace, which is so great we cannot understand it, will
keep your hearts and minds in Christ Jesus.

PHILIPPIANS 4:6-7 NCV

Dear God, it's easy to worry about things that feel out of my control. I need to remember everything is in your hands. Help me to pray more and worry less, so I can keep my heart and mind on you.

Are you worried about anything right now?

PURPOSE

You have been raised up with Christ.
So think about things that are in heaven.
That is where Christ is.
He is sitting at God's right hand.

COLOSSIANS 3:1 NIRV

We know that in all things God works
for the good of those who love him,
who have been called according to his purpose.

ROMANS 8:28 NIV

My child, pay attention to my words;
listen closely to what I say.
Don't ever forget my words;
keep them always in mind.

PROVERBS 4:20-21 NCV

Dear God, thank you that you have a great purpose for my life. Help me to walk closely with you, so I don't get distracted by other things. You want what is best for me and I trust you to show me what that is.

Can you think of what God might want you to do with your life?

COURTESY

Each of us should please our neighbors for their good,
to build them up. For even Christ did not please himself
but, as it is written: "The insults of those who insult you
have fallen on me."

ROMANS 15:2-3 NIV

See that no one pays back evil for evil,
but always try to do good to each other and to all people.

1 THESSALONIANS 5:15 NLT

Remind God's people to obey rulers and authorities.
Remind them to be ready to do what is good. Tell them
not to speak evil things against anyone. Remind them to
live in peace. They must consider the needs of others.
They must always be gentle toward everyone.

TITUS 3:1-2 NIRV

Dear God, I want to build others up and make them feel good. Help me to encourage my friends and think about them before myself. I pray also that I can be kind to strangers and help whoever is in need.

Can you think of an example of how you could show courtesy to a friend?

KINDNESS

Instead, be kind to each other, tenderhearted, forgiving
one another, just as God through Christ has forgiven you.

EPHESIANS 4:32 NLT

Kind people do themselves a favor,
but cruel people bring trouble on themselves.

PROVERBS 11:17 NCV

Do you disrespect God's great kindness and favor?
Do you disrespect God when he is patient with you?
Don't you realize that God's kindness
is meant to turn you away from your sins?

ROMANS 2:4 NIRV

Great is his love toward us,
and the faithfulness of the LORD endures forever.
Praise the LORD.

PSALM 117:2 NIV

Dear Jesus, your kindness is supposed to be an example for me to live by. It's not always easy to be kind, but that's how I can show your love to others. Help me to be more kind with my friends, family, and those who cross my path each day.

What is something kind you did for someone today?

REWARD

Remember that the Lord will give you an inheritance
as your reward, and that the Master you are serving
is Christ.

COLOSSIANS 3:24, NLT

"Love your enemies, do good to them, and lend to them
without expecting to get anything back. Then your
reward will be great, and you will be children of the Most
High, because he is kind to the ungrateful and wicked."

LUKE 6:35 NIV

Without faith it is impossible to please God. Those who
come to God must believe that he exists. And they must
believe that he rewards those who look to him.

HEBREWS 11:6 NIRV

Dear God, it is better to do good deeds without expecting anything in return. Help me to have that kind of attitude when helping others. I look forward to the reward you have for me in heaven.

Why is the attitude of serving without expecting something back important to God?

LEADERSHIP

The Lord's servant must not be quarrelsome but must be
kind to everyone, able to teach, not resentful. Opponents
must be gently instructed, in the hope that God will grant
them repentance leading them to a knowledge of the truth.

2 TIMOTHY 2:24-25 NIV

Do what is good. Set an example for them in everything.
When you teach, be honest and serious.

TITUS 2:7 NIRV

Without wise leadership, a nation falls;
there is safety in having many advisers.

PROVERBS 11:14 NLT

Dear Jesus, you are my leader, and I learn from you. It is good to have leaders in my life so I can learn to be a leader too. Help me to set a good example for others by showing them honesty and love.

In what ways are you a good leader?

FEAR

God gave us his Spirit. And the Spirit doesn't make us
weak and fearful. Instead, the Spirit gives us power and
love. He helps us control ourselves.

2 TIMOTHY 1:7 NIRV

The LORD is my light and my salvation—
whom shall I fear?
The LORD is the stronghold of my life—
of whom shall I be afraid?

PSALM 27:1 NIV

When I am afraid, I will trust you.
I praise God for his word.
I trust God, so I am not afraid.
What can human beings do to me?

PSALM 56:3-4 NCV

Dear God, I am afraid sometimes even though people say I don't need to be afraid. Help me to remember that you gave me a spirit of power and love so I don't have to fear anything.

What fears can you give to God right now?

FREEDOM

Now the Lord is the Spirit,
and where the Spirit of the Lord is,
there is freedom.

2 CORINTHIANS 3:17 NIV

My brothers and sisters, you were chosen to be free.
But don't use your freedom as an excuse to live in sin.
Instead, serve one another in love.

GALATIANS 5:13 NIRV

God did not give us a spirit that makes us afraid but a
spirit of power and love and self-control.

2 TIMOTHY 1:7 NCV

"If the Son sets you free, you are truly free."

JOHN 8:36 NLT

Dear God, it is a gift that I get to live in freedom and that I am able to do what I want. I pray that you change my heart so that what I want to do always honors you. Thank you for freedom!

How can you use your freedom to serve God?

JUSTICE

Do not try to punish others when they wrong you,
but wait for God to punish them with his anger.
It is written: "I will punish those who do wrong;
I will repay them," says the Lord.

ROMANS 12:19 NCV

He is the Rock. His works are perfect.
All his ways are right. He is faithful.
He doesn't do anything wrong.
He is honest and fair.

DEUTERONOMY 32:4 NIRV

The LORD secures justice for the poor
and upholds the cause of the needy.

PSALM 140:12 NIV

There is joy for those who deal justly with others
and always do what is right.

PSALM 106:3 NLT

Dear God, there is not always justice in this world, and sometimes that makes me mad. People who do bad things aren't always punished, and people who do good things sometimes get in trouble. Help me let go of my anger and let you be the perfect judge.

Why is God the best judge for the world?

CHANGE

"Unless you change and become like little children,
you will never enter the kingdom of heaven."

MATTHEW 18:3 NIV

Look! I tell you this secret:
We will not all sleep in death,
but we will all be changed.

1 CORINTHIANS 15:51 NCV

He will take our weak mortal bodies and change them
into glorious bodies like his own, using the same power
with which he will bring everything under his control.

PHILIPPIANS 3:21 NLT

Jesus Christ is the same yesterday and today and forever.

HEBREWS 13:8 NIRV

Dear God, change can be scary, like moving to a new house or going to a new school. But changing for you means being kind and generous and helpful to my friends and family. I want to make that kind of change. Thank you that you are perfect and you never change!

What kind of changes do you want to make for Jesus?

FORGIVENESS

"If you forgive other people when they sin against you,
your heavenly Father will also forgive you."

MATTHEW 6:14 NIV

Put up with each other.
Forgive one another if you are
holding something against someone.
Forgive, just as the Lord forgave you.

COLOSSIANS 3:13 NIRV

God is faithful and fair. If we confess our sins,
he will forgive our sins. He will forgive every wrong thing
we have done. He will make us pure.

1 JOHN 1:9 NIRV

He is so rich in kindness and grace that he purchased our
freedom with the blood of his Son and forgave our sins.

EPHESIANS 1:7 NLT

Dear God, forgiveness is not easy to give when I'm mad. I need to remember that I am not perfect either and that you forgive me daily. Help me to use you as my example.

Why is forgiveness so hard to give sometimes?

HAPPINESS

I will praise you, Lord, with all my heart.
I will tell all the miracles you have done.
I will be happy because of you; God Most High,
I will sing praises to your name.

PSALM 9:1-2 NCV

Lord, you alone are my inheritance, my cup of blessing.
You guard all that is mine.
The land you have given me is a pleasant land.
What a wonderful inheritance!

PSALM 16:5-6 NLT

Happiness makes a person smile,
but sadness can break a person's spirit.

PROVERBS 15:13 NCV

People should be happy and do good while they live.

ECCLESIASTES 3:12 NIRV

Dear God, I've learned that a happy heart is a thankful heart, so thank you for everything you've given me. I want to appreciate you and the life you've given me more from now on. Please help me to have a happier, more thankful attitude.

Is there anything you are especially happy about today?

HELP

My brothers and sisters, you will face all kinds of trouble.
When you do, think of it as pure joy. Your faith will be
tested. You know that when this happens it will produce
in you the strength to continue.

JAMES 1:2-3 NIRV

God will never forget the needy;
the hope of the afflicted will never perish.

PSALM 9:18 NIV

Take a new grip with your tired hands and strengthen
your weak knees. Mark out a straight path for your feet
so that those who are weak and lame will not fall but
become strong.

HEBREWS 12:12-14 NLT

"My grace is enough for you. When you are weak,
my power is made perfect in you."

2 CORINTHIANS 12:9 NCV

Dear God, there are things I cannot do alone, and that's how it should be. I should not rely on my own strength because I'm not strong enough to face the world without you. Thank you for helping me in my weakness.

What do you need God's help with?

ETERNITY

We are citizens of heaven,
where the Lord Jesus Christ lives.
And we are eagerly waiting for him
to return as our Savior.

PHILIPPIANS 3:20 NLT

"If I go and prepare a place for you, I will come back and
take you to be with me that you also may be where I am."

JOHN 14:3 NIV

That will happen in a flash, as quickly as you can wink
an eye. It will happen at the blast of the last trumpet.
Then the dead will be raised to live forever.
And we will be changed.

1 CORINTHIANS 15:52 NIRV

Surely your goodness and love will be with me all my life,
and I will live in the house of the LORD forever.

PSALM 23:6 NCV

Dear Jesus, eternity is a strange but cool concept. Because I have accepted you in my heart, I get to live forever with you. One day, you will come back for all of your children and that includes me! Thank you for this wonderful gift.

Can you think of something you would love to do forever?

ANXIETY

You will keep in perfect peace those
whose minds are steadfast,
because they trust in you.

ISAIAH 26:3 NIV

"Don't let your hearts be troubled.
Trust in God, and trust also in me."

JOHN 14:1 NLT

Give all your worries to him,
because he cares about you.

1 PETER 5:7 NCV

I call out to the LORD when I'm in trouble,
and he answers me.

PSALM 120:1 NIRV

Dear God, there are some things that make me anxious, but I know I need to learn to trust in you more. You care about me and my troubles. Help me to pray more and worry less.

What steps can you take to be less anxious and more trusting?

CREATIVITY

Lord, you have made many things;
with your wisdom you made them all.
The earth is full of your riches.

Psalm 104:24 NCV

For we are God's masterpiece. He has created us anew
in Christ Jesus, so we can do the good things he planned
for us long ago.

Ephesians 2:10 NLT

The Lord has filled him with the Spirit of God. He has
filled him with wisdom, with understanding, with
knowledge and with all kinds of skill.

Exodus 35:31 NIRV

We have different gifts,
according to the grace given to each of us.

Romans 12:6 NIV

Dear God, you made the whole world and everything in it. You are very creative to have put together so many different people, animals, and plants. Help me to be creative also with the gifts I have. I want to use my gifts for you.

How can you use your creativity for God?

LIFE

All praise to God, the Father of our Lord Jesus Christ.
It is by his great mercy that we have been born again,
because God raised Jesus Christ from the dead.
Now we live with great expectation.

1 PETER 1:3 NLT

That faith and that knowledge come from the hope
for life forever, which God promised to us
before time began.

TITUS 1:2 NCV

His divine power has given us everything we need for a
godly life through our knowledge of him who called us by
his own glory and goodness.

2 PETER 1:3 NIV

Dear Jesus, you gave your life for me. Now, I want to give my life to you. Help me to use what I've learned about you and your Word to live for you. Thank you for my life and the lives of everyone I love.

What is the best part of life?

PROTECTION

My God is my rock. I can run to him for safety.
He is my shield and my saving strength,
my defender and my place of safety.
The LORD saves me from those who want to harm me.

2 SAMUEL 22:3 NCV

The LORD keeps you from all harm
and watches over your life.
The LORD keeps watch over you as you come and go,
both now and forever.

PSALM 121:7-8 NLT

We are pushed hard from all sides. But we are not beaten
down. We are bewildered. But that doesn't make us lose
hope. Others make us suffer. But God does not desert us.
We are knocked down. But we are not knocked out.

2 CORINTHIANS 4:8-9 NIRV

Dear God, sometimes I think I'm strong and I don't need protection. That is not true though. I need you as my defender because this world tries to knock me down. Thank you for always watching over me.

How does it make you feel to know God is always protecting you?

UNDERSTANDING

Understanding is like a fountain of life
to those who have it.
But foolish people are punished
for the foolish things they do.

PROVERBS 16:22 NIRV

The teaching of your word gives light,
so even the simple can understand.

PSALM 119:130 NLT

Give me understanding,
so that I may keep your law and obey it with all my heart.

PSALM 119:34 NIV

Don't act thoughtlessly,
but understand what the Lord wants you to do.

EPHESIANS 5:17 NLT

Dear God, there are a lot of things I don't understand, but the more I learn about you and your Word, the more I will know. Help me to seek you in everything I do.

What do you need God to help you understand better?

COMPASSION

When I am with those who are weak, I share their
weakness, for I want to bring the weak to Christ.
Yes, I try to find common ground with everyone,
doing everything I can to save some.

1 CORINTHIANS 9:22 NLT

God, have mercy on me according to your faithful love.
Because your love is so tender and kind, wipe out my
lawless acts.

PSALM 51:1 NIRV

Praise be to the God and Father of our Lord Jesus Christ,
the Father of compassion and the God of all comfort.

2 CORINTHIANS 1:3 NIV

Dear Jesus, you are compassionate with me when I am weak. I hope others see me needing you when I have trouble. Help me to act with more love toward my friends and family so they can find your compassion as well.

How do you show compassion?

PRAISE

Sing to the LORD a new song,
his praise from the ends of the earth,
you who go down to the sea, and all that is in it,
you islands, and all who live in them.

ISAIAH 42:10 NIV

Praise the LORD from the skies.
Praise him high above the earth.
Praise him, all you angels.
Praise him, all you armies of heaven.
Praise him, sun and moon.
Praise him, all you shining stars.
Praise him, highest heavens
and you waters above the sky.
Let them praise the LORD,
because they were created by his command.

PSALM 148:1-5 NCV

Dear God, you deserve so much more praise than I can give. Even the sun and moon cannot give you enough praise. Thank you for all the blessings you have given me, and thank you for sending your Son to die for me.

How can you show God praise?

BELIEF

"God so loved the world that he gave his one and only
Son, that whoever believes in him shall not perish
but have eternal life."

JOHN 3:16 NIV

To all who believed him and accepted him,
he gave the right to become children of God.

JOHN 1:12 NLT

The message as it has been taught can be trusted. He
must hold firmly to it. Then he will be able to use true
teaching to comfort others and build them up. He will be
able to prove that people who oppose it are wrong.

TITUS 1:9 NIRV

Dear Jesus, I believe in you and am always wanting to learn more. Help me to share my belief with my friends who don't know you. I want to use what I know to defend your name if I ever need to.

How do you talk about what you believe?

DISCOURAGEMENT

"For I know the plans I have for you," declares the LORD,
"plans to prosper you and not to harm you,
plans to give you hope and a future."

JEREMIAH 29:11 NIV

"Come to me, all of you who are tired and have heavy
loads, and I will give you rest."

MATTHEW 11:28 NCV

This same God who takes care of me will supply all your
needs from his glorious riches, which have been given to
us in Christ Jesus.

PHILIPPIANS 4:19 NLT

Dear God, I sometimes feel discouraged when I don't do well on a test or in sports. You are there for me when I feel like I'm not good enough. I pray that I will ask for your help when I'm in need.

What could you use God's help with today?

GENEROSITY

Give generously to them and do so without a grudging
heart; then because of this the LORD your God will bless you
in all your work and in everything you put your hand to.

DEUTERONOMY 15:10 NIV

Each of you should give what you have decided in your
heart to give. You shouldn't give if you don't want to.
You shouldn't give because you are forced to.
God loves a cheerful giver.

2 CORINTHIANS 9:7 NIRV

If you help the poor, you are lending to the LORD—
and he will repay you!

PROVERBS 19:17 NLT

Dear God, I don't want to be selfish with my stuff. I want to give more to others. Help me to give with a generous heart instead of giving because I feel like I should. When I help others, I help show your love.

What is your favorite part of giving to others?

INTEGRITY

I know, my God, that you test the heart and are pleased
with integrity. All these things I have given willingly and
with honest intent.

1 Chronicles 29:17 niv

"If you ignore the least commandment and teach others
to do the same, you will be called the least in the Kingdom
of Heaven. But anyone who obeys God's laws and teaches
them will be called great in the Kingdom of Heaven."

Matthew 5:19 nlt

The honest person will live in safety,
but the dishonest will be caught.

Proverbs 10:9 ncv

Dear God, integrity means doing the right thing even when no one is looking. You are always watching, so you know when I make the right choice and when I slip and fall. Help me to be more honest and live with integrity.

In what ways can you show integrity?

BOLDNESS

He proclaimed the kingdom of God
and taught about the Lord Jesus Christ—
with all boldness and without hindrance!

ACTS 28:31 NIV

Sinners run away even when no one is chasing them.
But those who do what is right are as bold as lions.

PROVERBS 28:1 NIRV

On the day I called you, you answered me.
You made me strong and brave.

PSALM 138:3 NCV

Let us come boldly to the throne of our gracious God.
There we will receive his mercy, and we will find grace to
help us when we need it most.

HEBREWS 4:16 NLT

Dear God, you want me to be bold like a lion for you. I pray for confidence and strength when I try to talk about you with my friends. Help me work on speaking with boldness.

What helps you feel confident and bold?

DELIGHT

When I received your words, I ate them.
They filled me with joy. My heart took delight in them.
LORD God who rules over all, I belong to you.

JEREMIAH 15:16 NIRV

"My God, I want to do what you want.
Your teachings are in my heart."

PSALM 40:8 NCV

Your laws are my treasure;
they are my heart's delight.

PSALM 119:111 NLT

"Let your light shine before others, that they may see
your good deeds and glorify your Father in heaven."

MATTHEW 5:16 NIV

Dear Jesus, I am happy you are in my life. I hope the joy you give me is visible to my friends and family so they can know you too. Thank you for everything you've blessed me with.

How can you share God's delight with others?

COOPERATION

Make me truly happy by agreeing wholeheartedly with
each other, loving one another, and working together
with one mind and purpose.

PHILIPPIANS 2:2 NLT

Agree with one another. Don't be proud. Be willing to
be a friend of people who aren't considered important.
Don't think that you are better than others.

ROMANS 12:16 NIRV

Do not make friends with a hot-tempered person,
do not associate with one easily angered.

PROVERBS 22:24 NIV

Finally, all of you should be in agreement,
understanding each other,
loving each other as family,
being kind and humble.

1 PETER 3:8 NCV

Dear God, sometimes I think my ideas are better than other people's ideas, and it makes us fight. Help me to be open-minded and loving toward my friends and family so we can learn to work together and live in peace.

How could you cooperate better with your friends and family?

FAITH

Through Christ you have come to trust in God. And you
have placed your faith and hope in God because he raised
Christ from the dead and gave him great glory.

1 PETER 1:21 NLT

"Because your faith is much too small. What I'm about
to tell you is true. If you have faith as small as a mustard
seed, it is enough. You can say to this mountain, 'Move
from here to there.' And it will move. Nothing will be
impossible for you."

MATTHEW 17:20 NIRV

The important thing is faith—
the kind of faith that works through love.

GALATIANS 5:6 NCV

Faith is confidence in what we hope for and assurance
about what we do not see.

HEBREWS 11:1 NIV

Dear Jesus, it's crazy how powerful faith is. Faith means trusting you in my heart. It means you will forgive all of my sins and let me live with you in heaven. Help me to live for you and strengthen my faith each day.

What do you understand about faith?

DEVOTION

"Whoever wants to be my disciple must deny themselves and take up their cross and follow me."

MATTHEW 16:24 NIV

"No servant can serve two masters. The servant will hate one master and love the other, or will follow one master and refuse to follow the other. You cannot serve both God and worldly riches."

LUKE 16:13 NCV

Do your best to please God. Be a worker who doesn't need to be ashamed. Teach the message of truth correctly.

2 TIMOTHY 2:15 NIRV

Don't copy the behavior and customs of this world, but let God transform you into a new person by changing the way you think. Then you will learn to know God's will for you, which is good and pleasing and perfect.

ROMANS 12:2 NLT

Dear Jesus, I am devoted to you. I like to play games and watch movies, but I want to think and act like you. Help me to keep my focus on you so others can see my devotion and ask me about you.

How can you show others your devotion to Jesus?

QUIET

There is a time to tear apart and a time to sew together.
There is a time to be silent and a time to speak.

ECCLESIASTES 3:7 NCV

It is good to wait quietly for salvation from the LORD.

LAMENTATIONS 3:26 NLT

Those who are careful about what they say
keep themselves out of trouble.

PROVERBS 21:23 NIRV

Tremble and do not sin;
when you are on your beds,
search your hearts and be silent.

PSALM 4:4 NIV

Dear God, there is a lot of noise in this world, but there is time to talk and time to be silent. I want to hear you more in my life, so help me to learn when to be quiet.

How do you block out the noise of this world?

ANGER

Don't get angry.
Don't be upset; it only leads to trouble.
Evil people will be sent away,
but those who trust the LORD will inherit the land.

PSALM 37:8-9 NCV

Everyone should be quick to listen, slow to speak and slow to become angry, because human anger does not produce the righteousness that God desires.

JAMES 1:19-20 NIV

"Don't sin by letting anger control you." Don't let the sun go down while you are still angry,

EPHESIANS 4:26 NLT

Dear God, sometimes I feel really mad. I know it's not good to be angry, so please help me to cool my temper when I feel it getting out of control. I want to speak less and listen more so I can honor you better.

What helps you settle down when you're angry?

GUILT

The LORD and King helps me. He won't let me be
dishonored. So I've made up my mind to keep on serving
him. I know he won't let me be put to shame.

ISAIAH 50:7 NIRV

Those who go to him for help are happy,
and they are never disgraced.

PSALM 34:5 NCV

No, dear brothers and sisters, I have not achieved it, but
I focus on this one thing: Forgetting the past and looking
forward to what lies ahead.

PHILIPPIANS 3:13 NLT

Dear Jesus, I want your forgiveness so that I don't feel guilty. Help me to admit my sins and ask for your grace. After that, you say I should forget the past and focus on the future. I need you to help me do this.

Why doesn't God want you to feel guilt and shame?

TRUST

"I am the way and the truth and the life.
No one comes to the Father except through me."

JOHN 14:6 NIRV

Those who know the LORD trust him,
because he will not leave those who come to him.

PSALM 9:10 NCV

I trust in you, LORD. I say, "You are my God." My whole
life is in your hands.
Save me from the hands of my enemies. Save me from
those who are chasing me.

PSALM 31:14-15 NIV

Yes, the LORD is for me; he will help me.
I will look in triumph at those who hate me.
It is better to take refuge in the LORD than to trust in people.

PSALM 118:7-8 NLT

Dear Jesus, I know I can always trust you and that you are the way to eternal life. Help me to come to you when I have questions about my faith or I am afraid of something. I need you.

How do you know you can trust God?

GRACE

Let the words you speak always be full of grace. Learn how to make your words what people want to hear. Then you will know how to answer everyone.

COLOSSIANS 4:6 NIRV

God gives us even more grace, as the Scripture says, "God is against the proud, but he gives grace to the humble."

JAMES 4:6 NCV

Sin is no longer your master,
for you no longer live under the requirements of the law.
Instead, you live under the freedom of God's grace.

ROMANS 6:14 NLT

Dear Jesus, your grace gave me forgiveness and love. It's what allows me stay in relationship with you. Help me to act with more grace during my days so I can live like you.

How can you use grace when you are with others?

LONELINESS

"Teach them to obey everything that I have taught you, and
I will be with you always, even until the end of this age."

The LORD is near to all who call on him,

yes, to all who call on him in truth.

PSALM 145:18 NLT

Who can separate us from Christ's love?

Can trouble or hard times or harm or hunger?

Can nakedness or danger or war?

ROMANS 8:35 NIRV

"Be strong and courageous. Do not be afraid or terrified
because of them, for the LORD your God goes with you;
he will never leave you nor forsake you."

DEUTERONOMY 31:6 NIV

Dear God, when I'm alone, I know that I am never really alone. You are always with me. Thank you for being my courage and strength when I feel lost.

When do you feel lonely?

VICTORY

You can prepare a horse for the day of battle.
But the power to win comes from the Lord.

PROVERBS 21:31 NIRV

For every child of God defeats this evil world,
and we achieve this victory through our faith.

1 JOHN 5:4 NLT

From the Lord comes deliverance.
May your blessing be on your people.

PSALM 3:8 NIV

My dear brothers and sisters, I love you and want
to see you. You bring me joy and make me proud of you,
so stand strong in the Lord as I have told you.

PHILIPPIANS 4:1 NCV

Dear Jesus, no matter how prepared I feel for my challenges, I will never totally be ready without you. When I win games with my friends or do well in competitions, help me remember all victories come from you.

What is the last victory you had?

SALVATION

The wages of sin is death,
but the gift of God is eternal life
in Christ Jesus our Lord.

ROMANS 6:23 NIV

God's grace has saved you because of your faith in Christ.
Your salvation doesn't come from anything you do.
It is God's gift.

EPHESIANS 2:8 NIRV

If you openly declare that Jesus is Lord and believe in
your heart that God raised him from the dead,
you will be saved.

ROMANS 10:9 NLT

Dear Jesus, I want to give you my whole heart so I can always be with you. I am a sinner and I don't deserve your forgiveness, but you give it anyway. Thank you for dying on the cross for me.

What does salvation mean?

FAMILY

Jesus, who makes people holy, and those who are made holy are from the same family. So he is not ashamed to call them his brothers and sisters.

HEBREWS 2:11 NCV

As we have opportunity, let us do good to all people, especially to those who belong to the family of believers.

GALATIANS 6:10 NIV

So it is with Christ's body. We are many parts of one body, and we all belong to each other.

ROMANS 12:5 NLT

Dear God, if your family is anything like mine, it's crazy but awesome. Thank you for making me part of your family so I can be surrounded by people who love you.

What do you love about the family God has put you in?

COURAGE

Be strong in the Lord and in his mighty power.
Put on the full armor of God, so that you can take your
stand against the devil's schemes.

EPHESIANS 6:10-11 NIV

Be alert. Continue strong in the faith.
Have courage, and be strong. Do everything in love.

1 CORINTHIANS 16:13-14 NCV

Even though I walk through the darkest valley,
I will not be afraid. You are with me.

PSALM 23:4 NIRV

"This is my command—be strong and courageous!
Do not be afraid or discouraged.
For the LORD your God is with you wherever you go."

JOSHUA 1:9 NLT

Dear God, I'm not always brave enough to conquer my fears or to stand up for what I think, but you help me to have courage. Help me to keep learning your Word and doing your work with the armor you gave me.

When was the last time you showed courage?

PEACE

"I have told you these things, so that you can have peace
because of me. In this world you will have trouble.
But be encouraged! I have won the battle over the world."

JOHN 16:33 NIRV

The LORD gives his people strength.
The LORD blesses them with peace.

PSALM 29:11 NLT

Now may the Lord of peace himself give you peace at all
times and in every way. The Lord be with all of you.

2 THESSALONIANS 3:16 NIV

"I am leaving you with a gift—peace of mind and heart.
And the peace I give is a gift the world cannot give.
So don't be troubled or afraid."

JOHN 14:27 NLT

Dear God, I need to remember that you have given me the gift of peace. My life won't always be easy, but you say I never need to be afraid. Thank you for winning the battle for me.

When do you need to remember the peace God gave you?

LOVE

Three things will last forever—faith, hope, and love—
and the greatest of these is love.

1 CORINTHIANS 13:13 NLT

LORD, you are good. You are forgiving.
You are full of love for all who call out to you.

PSALM 86:5 NIRV

Fill us with your love every morning.
Then we will sing and rejoice all our lives.

PSALM 90:14 NCV

Let love and faithfulness never leave you;
bind them around your neck,
write them on the tablet of your heart.

PROVERBS 3:3 NIV

Dear Jesus, you teach me that love is an important characteristic. You don't just love when it's easy. You love all the time. I want to use your love as an example of how to love others.

How can you share some of God's love today?

CONFIDENCE

I can do everything through Christ,

who gives me strength.

PHILIPPIANS 4:13 NLT

Be my rock of refuge,

to which I can always go;

give the command to save me,

for you are my rock and my fortress....

You have been my hope, Sovereign LORD,

my confidence since my youth.

PSALM 71:3, 5 NIV

The LORD will be at your side.

He will keep your feet from being caught in a trap.

PROVERBS 3:26 NIRV

Dear God, I don't always feel confident enough to talk to new people or answer questions in large groups, but I know you are there for me. You give me the confidence I need. Thank you for being my strength.

Describe a time when God helped you feel more confident.

HONESTY

Keep me from deceitful ways;
be gracious to me and teach me your law.
I have chosen the way of faithfulness;
I have set my heart on your laws.

PSALM 119:29-30 NIV

"Everything that is hidden will become clear,
and every secret thing will be made known."

LUKE 8:17 NCV

The king is pleased with words from righteous lips;
he loves those who speak honestly.

PROVERBS 16:13 NLT

We will speak the truth in love.

EPHESIANS 4:15 NIRV

Dear Jesus, I want to be like you and follow your laws. Honesty is important. Help me to always be truthful to my family and friends. Thank you for your example.

Is there anything you need to be honest about?

ENCOURAGEMENT

The LORD your God is with you;
the mighty One will save you.
He will rejoice over you.
You will rest in his love;
he will sing and be joyful about you.

ZEPHANIAH 3:17 NCV

Encourage one another daily,
as long as it is called "Today."

HEBREWS 3:13 NIV

Kind words are like honey—
sweet to the soul and healthy for the body.

PROVERBS 16:24 NLT

Be joyful. Grow to maturity. Encourage each other.
Live in harmony and peace.
Then the God of love and peace will be with you.

2 CORINTHIANS 13:11 NLT

Dear God, it is true that kind words feel good and make the day better. Thank you for that reminder. Help me to encourage my friends and family like you encourage me.

What encourages you when you feel down?

DETERMINATION

In a race all the runners run. But only one gets the prize.
You know that, don't you? So run in a way that will get you
the prize. All who take part in the games train hard. They
do it to get a crown that will not last. But we do it to get a
crown that will last forever.

1 CORINTHIANS 9:24-25 NIRV

I have tried hard to find you—
don't let me wander from your commands.

PSALM 119:10 NLT

I have fought the good fight,
I have finished the race,
I have kept the faith.

2 TIMOTHY 4:7 NCV

Dear God, you want me to use determination to get the prize. I want to win because living forever in heaven with you is my prize. Help me to make it to the finish line for you.

How does winning for God make you feel?

LIGHT

"I am the light of the world. Whoever follows me will
never walk in darkness, but will have the light of life."

JOHN 8:12 NIV

"You are the light of the world—like a city on a hilltop that
cannot be hidden. No one lights a lamp and then puts
it under a basket. Instead, a lamp is placed on a stand,
where it gives light to everyone in the house. In the same
way, let your good deeds shine out for all to see, so that
everyone will praise your heavenly Father."

MATTHEW 5:14-16 NLT

At one time you were in the dark. But now you are
in the light because of what the Lord has done.
Live like children of the light.

EPHESIANS 5:8 NIRV

Dear Jesus, you are the light that can't be covered. I want to have that light too and show others how amazing you are. It's not so easy when the world is so dark, but when I trust in you, I am confident.

How can you be a light for God?

PRAYER

LORD, in the morning you hear my voice.
In the morning I pray to you.
I wait for you in hope.

PSALM 5:3 NIRV

Never stop praying.

1 THESSALONIANS 5:17 NIRV

The LORD does not listen to the wicked,
but he hears the prayers of those who do right.

PROVERBS 15:29 NCV

Come, let us bow down in worship,
let us kneel before the LORD our Maker.

PSALM 95:6 NIV

Dear God, sometimes I don't talk to you as much as I should. You want to hear from me when good and bad things happen in my life. Help me to never stop praying. Thank you for hearing me whenever I speak.

What can you pray about right now?

DISOBEDIENCE

Children, obey your parents in everything,
for this pleases the Lord.

COLOSSIANS 3:20 NIV

Even children are known by their behavior;
their actions show if they are innocent and good.

PROVERBS 20:11 NCV

Those who keep commandments keep their lives.
But those who don't care how they live will die.

PROVERBS 19:16 NIRV

Remember, it is sin to know what you ought to do
and then not do it.

JAMES 4:17 NLT

Dear God, sometimes I know what I should do, but I don't do it. And sometimes I know what I shouldn't do and do it anyway. That is disobedience, and I don't want to act that way. Help me to obey my parents and you.

Why is it important to be obedient?

HELPFULNESS

"In everything I did, I showed you that by this kind of
hard work we must help the weak, remembering the
words the Lord Jesus himself said: 'It is more blessed to
give than to receive.'"

ACTS 20:35 NIV

"Who is more important? Is it the one at the table, or the
one who serves? Isn't it the one who is at the table?
But I am among you as one who serves."

LUKE 22:27 NIRV

Share with God's people who need help.
Bring strangers in need into your homes.

ROMANS 12:13 NCV

Dear Jesus, it feels good to receive help and gifts, but you say it is better to serve others instead. That is a good reminder. Help me to have a heart for people who have less than I do.

What is something helpful you could do for someone today?

BroadStreet Kids
BroadStreet Kids is an imprint of BroadStreet Publishing Group, LLC.
Racine, Wisconsin, USA
Broadstreetpublishing.com

PRAYERS & PROMISES FOR BOYS

ISBN 978-1-4245-5416-4 (faux)
ISBN 978-1-4245-5417-1 (ebook)

Design by Chris Garborg | garborgdesign.com
Compiled by Kendall Moon.
Edited by Michelle Winger.

Printed in China.

17   18   19   20   21   22   23   7   6   5   4   3   2   1